D0331423

Savage, Jeff
Getting ready for a career
in professional sports

SEP 1 1 1996

**DO NOT REMOVE
CARDS FROM POCKET**

**ALLEN COUNTY PUBLIC LIBRARY
FORT WAYNE, INDIANA 46802**

You may return this book to any agency, branch,

or bookmobile of the Allen County Public Library.

DEMCO

# A Career in...

# Professional Sports

by Jeff Savage

Illustrated with photographs
by Peter Ford

Capstone Press

MINNEAPOLIS

Allen County Public Library
900 Webster Street
PO Box 2270
Fort Wayne, IN 46801-2270

Copyright © 1996 Capstone Press. All rights reserved. No part of this book may be reproduced in any form without written permission from the publisher.

Printed in the United States of America.

Capstone Press • 2440 Fernbrook Lane • Minneapolis, MN 55447

Editorial Director    John Coughlan
Managing Editor      Tom Streissguth
Production Editor     James Stapleton
Book Design    Tim Halldin

**Library of Congress Cataloging-in-Publication Data**
Savage, Jeff, 1961--
    A career in-- professional sports / Jeff Savage.
      p. cm.
    Includes bibliographical references (p. 43) and index.
    Summary: Provides brief descriptions of various jobs connected with professional sports, including athlete, coach, official, marketing, and team management.
    ISBN 1-56065-293-4
    1. Sports--Vocational guidance--Juvenile literature. [1. Sports--Vocational guidance. 2. Occupations.] I. Title.
    GV734.S28    1996
    796'.023--dc20                              95-19377
                                                CIP
                                                AC

# Table of Contents

# Chapter 1

# Working in Professional Sports

The San Diego Chargers are about to play the San Francisco 49ers in the 1995 Super Bowl. Thousands of fans are packed into Joe Robbie Stadium in Miami, Florida. Millions more are watching on television.

Bill Johnston is standing on the Chargers sideline. Keoki Kamau crouches nearby. Bill and Keoki are not football players. Bill is a

**Working as a sports camera operator will put you right next to the action.**

public-relations director. He gives **statistics** and other information to writers and broadcasters. His work helps the members of the **media** describe the game to the public. Keoki is a trainer. He wraps players with tape and bandages and helps them if they get hurt.

When the game begins, Bill goes to the **press box** with the reporters. Keoki stays on the sideline with the players. Bill and Keoki grew up with a love of sports. They worked hard in school, and they used their skills and experience to find good jobs. Now they are on the field at the Super Bowl.

Sports today is a big industry. It employs thousands of people in all sorts of jobs. Fans go to games to see superstar athletes, such as Deion Sanders, Barry Bonds, and Shaquille O'Neal. But sports also has coaches, lawyers, engineers, ushers, equipment managers, secretaries, reporters, and scouts. Managers, sportscasters, scoreboard operators, umpires, and referees all work during the games, making sure that the contest goes smoothly.

Many young sports fans dream of becoming professional athletes. There is nothing wrong with dreaming. But the odds against success are very high. If you don't have the chance to play with the pros, you can still earn a living in professional sports. In this book, you will read about a few of the hundreds of sports-related occupations. There may be one that fits your interests and abilities—and keeps you close to the game.

**Promotions staffers arrange special events for the team.**

# Chapter 2

# Jobs in Pro Sports

Here are some of the jobs available today in the sports field.

## Athlete

Whether they play hockey, football, tennis, or golf, many pro athletes earn huge amounts of money. For instance, the average salary for a baseball player today is more than $1 million a year.

But it takes natural ability and luck to become a professional athlete. It also takes a lot of hard work. An athlete must maintain a well-conditioned body at all times or risk

**Professional athletes must work constantly to stay in condition and to keep their skills sharp.**

serious injury. He or she spends hours in the gym or in the workout room. Athletes exercise, lift weights, jog, and run sprints. Their jobs are not all fun and games.

A college education is not necessary, but more than half of all pro athletes have one. Nearly all football and basketball players, for instance, must prove their ability in college in order to be **drafted** to the pros.

How many jobs are available? Here are some numbers to consider. There are 1,290 National Football League players at any given time. There are 672 major-league baseball players, and 324 players in the National Basketball Association.

Only the best 200 or so golfers in the world compete on the Professional Golfers' Association tour. That number is about the same for pro tennis players, horse-racing jockeys, auto-racing drivers, and most other sports. With such limited numbers of available jobs, the chances of working as a paid athlete are small.

## Coach

Every pro sports team has a coach. Even athletes of non-team sports such as golf and tennis have a coach. The success of a team or individual depends largely on the coaching staff.

Team coaches have many duties. During practice, they design plays and teach athletes

3 1833 02947 9620

the finer points of the sport. During the game, they plan strategy, give pep talks, and make decisions that could affect who wins and loses. They prepare the athletes to compete, both physically and mentally.

Some coaches go by other names. A head baseball coach, for example, is called a manager. He decides when to replace a pitcher, when to use a pinch-hitter, when to intentionally walk a batter, and when to steal, bunt, or swing away. On the field, line coaches stand just outside the playing area and give directions to runners and batters.

A football coach decides when to call time out and when to have his players run, pass, or punt. A hockey coach chooses the right mix of skaters to get the winning goal. Similarly, a basketball coach finds the right blend of athletes and designs the winning play.

**A baseball line coach gives directions on the field.**

Coaches work long hours during the season. Fortunately, they have assistants to help them. A head football coach has at least eight assistants, each in charge of a specific part of the team. A baseball manager has four coaches to help him. Hockey and basketball teams each have two or three assistants.

**Team mascots entertain the fans.**

Although formal education is not required of coaches, many jobs require at least a **bachelor's degree**. A complete understanding of the sport is crucial, too. The ability to handle players is very important for a coach in any sport.

Most coaches get to the pros by winning. They might start at the high school level, climb to the college ranks, and then move up to the pros. Others may be former star athletes who know the secrets of winning. No matter how they get to the top, they won't stay long if they don't win.

There are far fewer professional coaches than athletes. Coaches don't have to stay in top physical condition, nor do they need to excel at playing the game. But competition for jobs is intense, and the odds of becoming a coach are not very good.

## Officials

Games cannot be played without officials. They enforce the rules, make quick decisions, and keep order.

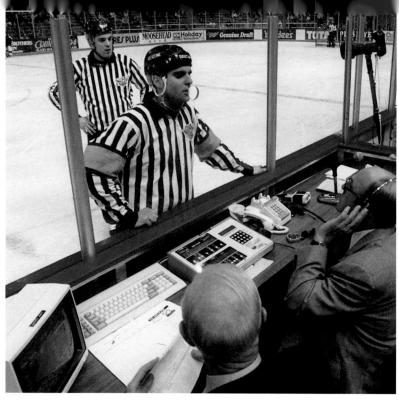

**During a professional hockey match, a referee talks over a play with the game's official scorer.**

A baseball game has four umpires. A football game uses a referee and six officials. A basketball game has three referees. There is a referee in boxing, a referee and two **linesmen** in hockey, a **chair umpire** and several linesmen in tennis, and a dozen course officials in golf.

These officials must know the rules of their sport. In team sports, they should know the different plays and formations. They must be honest and impartial. They cannot secretly root for one side or the other.

Baseball umpires and basketball referees are true professionals who are paid a full-time

**A baseball umpire rules on a play.**

salary. That is because there are 162 baseball games and 82 basketball games during the long regular seasons. Tennis and boxing have full-time officials, too.

The NFL has only 16 regular-season games. Except for the 14 referees, football officials are part-time employees. They work as dentists or bankers, or they have other occupations when they are not officiating the games.

Most officials attend a special school to learn their trade. In baseball, for instance, there are several winter-long umpire schools. From there, umpires join the minor leagues with the hope of one day breaking into the majors.

Officiating can be difficult and rewarding at the same time. It isn't easy hearing the complaints of coaches or the boos of angry fans. But it is exciting to be in the center of the action, and to know that your call could decide the game's outcome.

At a management meeting, important decisions are made about the team's future.

## Management

Managing a professional sports franchise requires a great deal of work at many levels. Coaches and players are too busy to decide what athlete to trade or what hotel to stay in. Those decisions and many others are left to team management.

The general manager oversees the basic operation of the team. He is responsible for the hiring and firing of coaches, players, and other employees. He also decides on the drafting and trading of players, the salaries to be paid, and dozens of other matters.

It takes many years to become a general manager, and there is no sure pathway to success in the field. Many general managers start by working with a school team while in high school or college.

Scouts judge the talent of high school and college players and report to the general manager. They also must evaluate upcoming opponents for the coaches. All professional teams employ several full-time scouts who are paid to watch games at all levels.

An equipment manager handles a team's sports equipment. He makes sure each piece of equipment fits the player, knows how to repair the equipment at a moment's notice, and oversees the shipping of the equipment from city to city.

A clubhouse or locker room manager takes care of the day-to-day operations in the team's

**dressing room**. He provides food, uniforms, and towels to the players, and delivers messages to them from their family or from fans.

Just like athletes, managers and scouts move up to the pros by gaining experience at lower levels. A college education is not required.

### Operations

It takes hundreds of people to operate such stadiums as Los Angeles Memorial Coliseum, Three Rivers Stadium in Pittsburgh, or

**During the game, concessions workers serve food and drinks to the fans.**

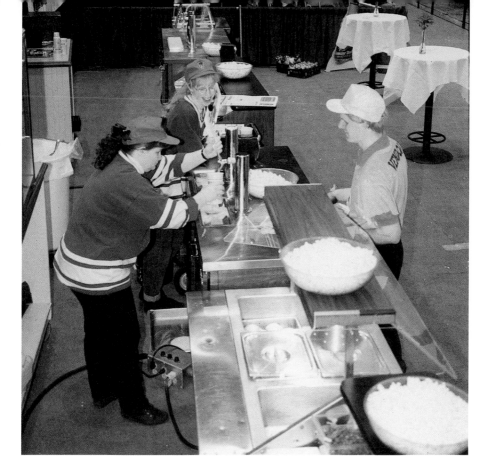

SkyDome in Toronto. And just as teams are managed, stadiums and arenas must be managed as well. This is the job of the facility operations staff.

Here are just some of the jobs in the operations department:

Facility maintenance workers oversee the lighting, plumbing, electricity, and other parts of the building.

Groundskeepers take care of the grass or artificial turf field. Food service workers prepare and distribute food and drinks. Ticket operators print and distribute tickets. Security personnel maintain order and keep fans away from players.

There are several full-time jobs in each of these areas and hundreds of part-time jobs. Vendors, who sell peanuts and hot dogs, and

**Members of the ground crew have to keep the playing field in good condition.**

ushers, who take tickets and escort fans to their seats, are usually part-time workers.

A college education is not needed for these jobs. New workers will receive on-the-job training.

Each facility also has a scoreboard operator and a public address announcer. Many of these professionals receive their training as assistants.

The hundreds of facility operations workers are busy during the games, but they always manage to sneak a peek at the action. The prospects of getting a job in this area are good.

## Marketing and Public Relations

Sports teams would be nothing without the fans. And fans wouldn't know about the teams if it weren't for the people involved in **marketing** and **promotions.**

The team's marketing staff, for example, might take charge of producing a television commercial to promote an upcoming home stand. The promotion staff finds ways to lure fans to the stadium or arena, usually through special events and giveaways.

Working on a marketing or promotions staff can be a lot of fun. To land one of these jobs, applicants should have at least a college degree.

It is important for teams and athletes to relate well with the public and the media. This is the responsibility of customer-relations and public-relations departments.

The customer-relations staff handles everything from special requests for tickets to general complaints. It provides information about upcoming games, seating, and ticket

**Customer-relations workers sell tickets and give information to fans over the phone.**

prices. It also may provide emergency first aid during a game.

The public relations (PR) staff makes sure athletes are available for interviews. It also produces game **programs** and fact-filled **media guides**. The relationship between athletes and the media is important, and the PR staff is a vital tool to maintain smooth relations.

Working in the customer relations or public relations departments requires good communications skills. Jobs are readily available, but a college degree is preferred.

There are also jobs available in the sports advertising business. Athletes are so popular that companies like to use them to promote their products. For instance, a potato-chip company might want to show Emmitt Smith eating its chips on national TV. This would require the work of a sports advertising agency.

Workers at the agency would make the arrangements to shoot a professionally made commercial, write the script, secure the rights to use the athlete, and make sure that everyone gets paid.

Sports advertising is a growing and wide-open field. Hundreds of new employees enter the field every year. Most agencies require them to have a college degree.

## Media

The members of the media tell the story of the game and the teams to the public. Working in the media can be a challenging and rewarding experience. But it is not easy. There is a lot of pressure to perform. Mistakes are not tolerated and competition is fierce.

Sportswriters arrive several hours before a game to talk with coaches and athletes. They look for stories or bits of information they

**Radio broadcasters have to give a vivid description of the game to their listeners.**

think the public will find interesting. During the game, they take careful notes that can be used in a story. Afterward, they get players' reactions to the match.

Then the serious work begins. The writer must create an interesting, informative, and entertaining story. If the game is played at night, he or she may have an hour or less to write the story. The story cannot be late.

Sportscasters are not under **deadline** pressure like newspaper sportswriters. But they have their own share of challenges.

Sportscasters also arrive before the game to visit with the players. They must be well-informed before the game, when they pass information on to the fans. The information must be interesting–and correct. Sportscasters must describe the action clearly and accurately. Radio announcers must be especially

**Photographers must have the right equipment, and fast reflexes, to catch the game's action.**

descriptive, because listeners cannot see what is happening.

Other media members include magazine writers, editors, photographers, TV cameramen, and electronic experts. There are thousands of media jobs. Each pro team's games are covered by local radio and television

**Sportscasters work in teams of two or three. Play-by-play announcers describe the game, and color commentators give their opinion of the action.**

**Television directors control camera shots during a game.**

stations that employ sportscasters. Small-town newspapers might have two sportswriters, while major newspapers employ 20 or more.

Two keys to getting a job in the media and working up the ladder are knowledge and experience. A thorough knowledge of teams, players, and coaches is essential. Working at a small newspaper or local radio station is a good way to start.

## Medical Staff

With sports come injuries. A team's medical staff works to keep athletes healthy.

Every athlete has met his team doctor at one time or another. The lucky ones just visit the doctor for regular checkups. But others must go through **surgery** or treatment for an injury.

Sports teams have several other medical staff members as well. An **orthopedic surgeon** often is available to assist the team doctor in

**Professional sports can test the body's limits. Sometimes, the result is an injury that the team doctor must treat.**

complex surgeries. An eye doctor and dentist also work with the team.

A trainer travels with the team during the season and has many tasks. Before the game, he or she helps athletes prevent injury by applying protective bandages and tape to sore spots. During the game, the trainer treats minor injuries on the field, the bench, or in the locker room. After the game, the trainer treats injuries in the trainer's room or assists the team physician with major injuries. After surgery, he or she manages the day-to-day treatment of the athletes.

Every sports team has a trainer. A college degree in physical therapy is required, and a master's degree is preferred.

The final member of a team's medical staff is the physical therapist. An athlete who undergoes surgery must be nursed back to health. The physical therapist guides the athlete through a series of exercises to regain strength and flexibility. To land a job, physical therapists must earn a college degree.

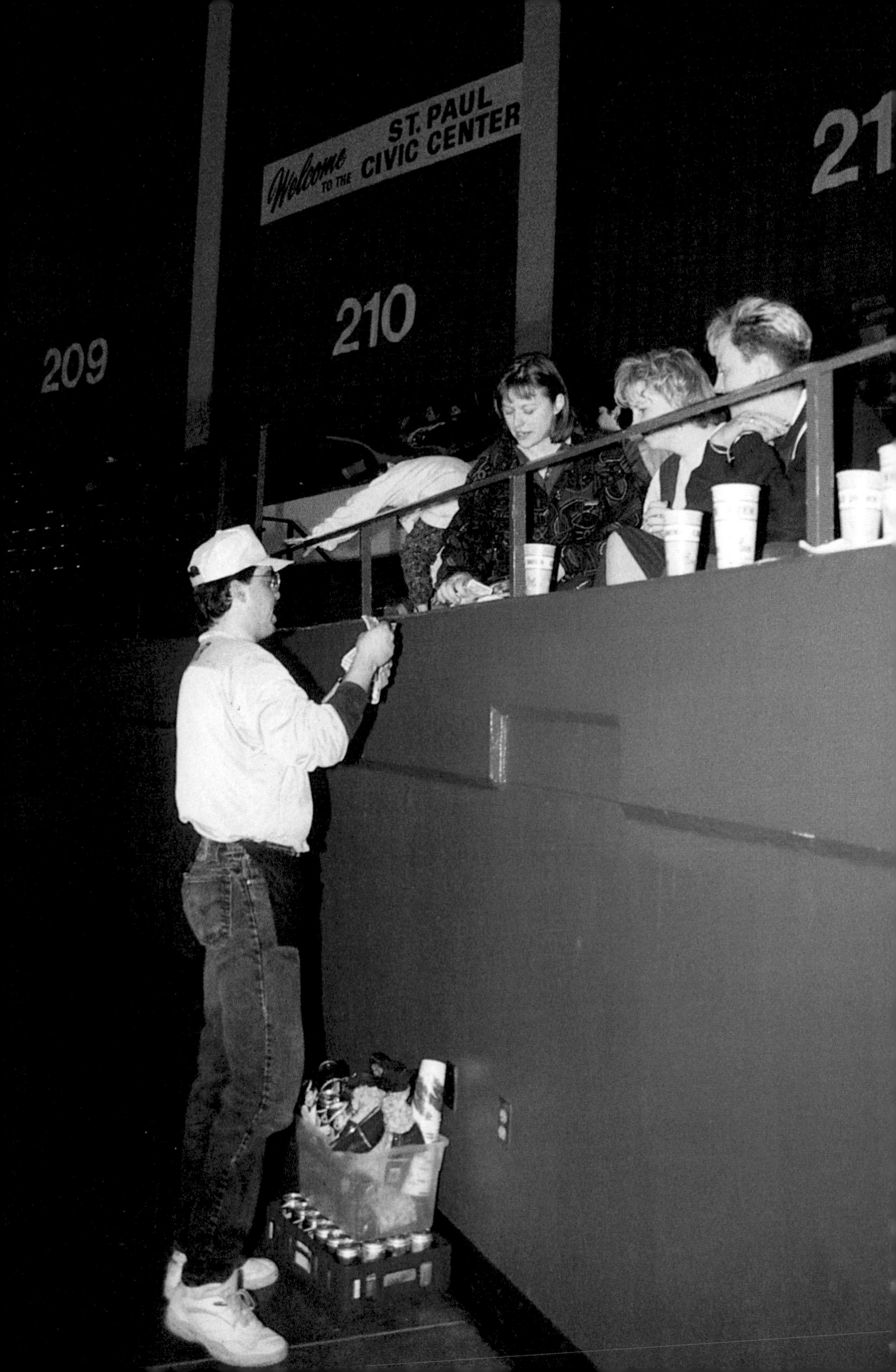

Welcome TO THE ST. PAUL CIVIC CENTER
209
210
21

# Chapter 3

# Getting Ready

Here are some ways to prepare for a future career in sports.

*Play.* Try out for sports teams at school and in your community. If you make the team. you will learn about the game as well as about physical fitness, diet, and training. Play and practice as often as you can.

**Vendors and other operations crew mix work with the fun of seeing athletes in action.**

*Read.* Plan your own personal reading program for background information about a sports career. Ask a librarian at your school or public library to help you find information on sports. Begin studying now. Read magazines and newspapers as well as books.

**The stadium's sound-board operator takes care of announcements, music, and special effects during a sports event.**

*Watch.* Attend sporting events at school and in the community. Try to attend games at all levels, from grade-school contests to the pros. Watch games on television and listen to the radio. Pay attention to how the good players and sucessful coaches handle themselves.

*Talk.* Ask questions of your friends, family, and people involved in sports. Talk to players, coaches, trainers, and anyone who knows about sports. When you attend games, talk to the people working at the stadium. Find out how they got started. Talk to coaches at your school and get their advice.

*Keep a notebook.* Write down useful phone numbers and addresses. Keep track of who's who in your local sports community.

Professional sports continues to gain in popularity. The many types of jobs available today will also be around in the future. Maybe one of these jobs will be yours.

# Glossary

**bachelor's degree**–a title usually earned after spending the first four years at a college or university

**chair umpire**–the official who controls tennis matches. Chair umpires work from a tall chair placed on the sideline.

**deadline**–the day or time that a job must be finished

**drafted**–to be selected by a team as one of the players

**dressing room**–the area where players get ready for the game by dressing and preparing their equipment

**linesman**–a hockey referee who watches the action for violations of the rules. The linesman works with the referee, who decides how to apply the rules to each situation.

**marketing**–the job of presenting and selling the products of a team or other organization to the public

**media**–the people and organizations that deliver written and broadcast information to the public

**media guide**–a booklet that gives information about the team to members of the media

**orthopedic surgeon**–a doctor who specializes in the treatment of injuries

**press box**–the area where sportswriters watch the game, take notes, and work on articles about the game

**programs**–guides to the teams and players that help the fans follow the action of the game

**promotions**–the job of organizing special events or giveaways that will attract the public to a game

**statistics**–information about the games, the teams, and the players

**surgery**–repairing an injury or illness with a medical operation

# To Learn More

**Downes, Paul.** *Chronicle Sports Careers.*
Moravia, N.Y.: Chronicle Guidance
Publications, 1991.

**Heitzmann, William R.** *Careers for Sports
Nuts.* Lincolnwood, Ill.: National Texbook
Co., 1990.

**Kaplan, Andrew.** *Careers for Outdoor Types.*
Millbrook Press, 1991.

**Kaplan, Andrew.** *Careers for Sports Fans.*
Millbrook Press, 1991.

**Nelson, Cordner.** *Careers in Pro Sports.* New
York: The Rosen Publishing Group, 1990.

# Some Useful Addresses

**American Alliance for Health, Physical Education, Recreation, and Dance**
1900 Association Drive
Reston, VA 22091

**American Sports Education Institute**
200 Castlewood Drive
North Palm Beach, FL 33408

**Canadian Sport and Fitness Administration Centre**
1600 James Naismith Drive
Gloucester ON K1B 5N4

**Federation of Professional Athletes**
2021 L St. NW
Washington, D.C. 20036

**National Athletic Trainers Association**
2952 Stemmons Freeway, Suite 200
Dallas, Texas 75247

**National Sporting Goods Association**
Lake Center Plaza Building
1699 Wall Street
Mount Prospect, IL  60056

**Sports Foundation**
Lake Center Plaza Building
1699 Wall Street
Mount Prospect, IL  60056

# Index